AIRDRIE

A BRIEF HISTORICAL SKETCH
FOR THE
TER-JUBILEE OF THE BURGH
1971

GEORGE THOMSON

AIRDRIE
TER-JUBILEE COMMITTEE
1971

Printed by George Outram & Co. Ltd., 46-50 Graham Street, Airdrie.

CONTENTS

ILLUSTRATIONS

ILLUSTRATIONS (Continued)

BEFORE 1821

The written history of our district began when some time between 1162 and 1164, as closely as we can date it, Malcolm IV added to the possessions of the Cistercian monks of Newbattle the lands that were to become known by 1323 as the Monklands.

Little or nothing is known of the social and economic development of the district throughout the next two centuries but towards the end of the fifteenth century there is definite evidence of the existence of a tenantry holding their lands either on lease or in steilbow*: from 1503 the lands of Airdrie were held by the Hamiltons on three successive 19-year leases; other examples could be cited.

General feuing out of the Monklands began after the complete destruction of the buildings of Newbattle Abbey in 1544 by an English army under the Earl of Hertford. One of the early charters was that of the lands of Airdrie granted to Methusalem Hamilton in 1559.

At first development proceeded slowly. In 1605 there occurs the first reference to Airdrietoun but no evidence of the number of its inhabitants is available until 1650. By that time the population of the eastern part of the Monklands had so increased that in January 1650 a new Parish of East or New Monkland was disjoined, its extent defined not by geographical boundaries but simply by naming the estates to be included in it. Against the name of each estate was set down the number of *communicants* living there and so we get a picture — a rather unexpected one — of the distribution of population within the parish of New Monkland at that time. Airdrie had 51 communicants, Gartlea 5, and Rochsolloch 14, a total of 70. In contrast Cromlet, Kipbyre and Kipps together accounted for 94; Myvet and Medrox for 152; East and West Blairlinns for 108; Glenhove and East and West Glentores for 120; Rochsoles, Inchnock, Gain and Gartmillan for 181; Ryding for 93. The complete enumeration has not been given here but it is quite evident that the greatest concentration of population was to the north of Airdrie. And so the site for New Monkland church was chosen north of Airdrie.

*When lands were held in steilbow, the owner provided his tenants with all that was necessary for working the lands — tools, implements, draught oxen and other animals. All these had to be returned at the end of the tenancy. In addition, of course, annual payments in cash and kind were made by the tenant.

Methusalem Hamilton had long been gathered to his fathers when in 1688 his great-great-grandson, Robert Hamilton, succeeded to the estate of Airdrie. By procuring in 1695 an Act of Parliament constituting Airdrie a market town with a weekly market and four fairs each year, Robert Hamilton made Airdrie a focus of interest and of trade for an area that extended far beyond the Monklands. Thus he laid the foundation of Airdrie's future prosperity.

In the closing decades of the seventeenth century he began to give off feus for housebuilding, first of all, it is said, in the Aitchison Street area. About 1720 some building took place in the vicinity of the Old Cross. The intervening space in Aitchison Street and High Street was more or less built up by 1755 and building had spread from the Old Cross down the South Loan and down the North Loan towards the Common. As yet there was very little building eastwards from the Old Cross. Building in Hallcraig began in the 1750s and in Wellwynd and Bell Street (Finnie's Lane) just after 1760. An enumeration made in 1755 assigned Airdrie 1,200 inhabitants. Forty years later it was estimated that the population had doubled. Of Rochsolloch House it had been said in 1771 that it was 'within a quarter of a mile of Airdry where every necessary for a family may be got in a moment's warning'. Airdrietoun was evidently growing in importance.

In 1774 John Aitchison, owner since 1770 of the lands of Airdrie, was advertising for a blacksmith 'for the town of Airdrie'. There had been established on Airdrie's South Burn between our Central Park and Stirling Street (then not envisaged) Airdrie Grain Mill, a brewery at the foot of the South Loan, a distillery on the gushet between Mill Street and Hallcraig Street, and on the site now occupied by the Public Library another brewery together with a sugar of lead manufactory, a waulk mill and a dyehouse. (Hence the Dyesters Bridge that carries Stirling Street over the South Burn.) And in 1783 James Kirkwood came from Glasgow to start, near the top of Bell Street, an iron foundry that was later taken over by John Dick and became one of our best-known engineering works in the nineteenth century.

But Airdrie was not to become noted for its engineering until the second half of the nineteenth century. Rather it was as a weaving community that it first gained fame. By mid-eighteenth century handloom weaving of woollen and linen fabrics was well-established. In 1770 John Balloch of Airdrie was advertising in the *Glasgow Journal* the grand art found out by him, of 'working with five treadles what formerly would require fifteen'. Airdrie Weavers Society was founded in 1781. Zacharias Anderson, one of Balloch's former apprentices, became its first Preses. His indentures, dated December, 1759, are preserved in Airdrie Public Library. At that time flax was being

THE NORTH LOAN

grown on 16 farms within the present bounds of the burgh. If the number is surprising the names are no less so: Airdrie, Hallcraig, Flowerhill, Drumbathie, Colliertree, Bellsdyke, Monkland, Petersburn, Bankhead, Cowbrae, Craigneuk, Mavisbank, Mosside, Kipbyre, Holehills and Rawyards. In 1786 weaving of cotton fabrics began to supplant that of native linens in Airdrie and just before 1800 an abortive attempt was made to start cotton spinning by machinery in a works associated with the waulk mill at the foot of Wellwynd.

In the last decade of the eighteenth century coal mining was in progress at Mavisbank, Whinhall, Kipbyre and Colliertree, all now within the Burgh. In all only 25 to 30 colliers were employed: even at 3d a cwt. coal was too expensive a fuel for most domestic users and Airdrie's feuars, however small their feu, had the prescriptive right to win peats from the moss to the north-east of the town.

A hundred years after the erection of Airdrie into a market town a further impetus was given to its development by the opening in May-June, 1795 of a new road between Glasgow and Edinburgh passing through Airdrie and Bathgate. This road was to become the main street of the town. Airdrie's 'New Town' began to appear by development along this new thoroughfare and the cross streets that were made linking it with the 'King's

Highway' that ran roughly parallel with it.* Very soon after the
road was completed it began to be used by regular stage coach
services between the two cities. At the Airdrie Inn (later the
Royal Hotel and still later the Royal Buildings) horses were
changed for the second stage of the journey to the Craig Inn
which still stands at Blackridge. Airdrie Inn with its stabling for
forty horses had been built by Andrew Stirling of Drumpellier,
chairman of the Road Trustees responsible for the Airdrie-
Bathgate section of the road. With enviable foresight the Trustees
had the road constructed of a width that has so far proved
adequate. Indeed an earlier generation could recall seeing
showmen parked on it during Airdrie Fairs.

To help in the upkeep of the road, users other than
pedestrians had to pay tolls at toll bars or turnpikes erected at
intervals along the road, often at points where side roads entered,
as at the Biggar Road crossing. In the 1790's the only north and
south road of any significance in Airdrie was this Biggar Road,
made in the seventeenth century by the Flemings, Earls of
Wigton, to link their lands of Cumbernauld with their main
estates at Biggar. When it was supplanted some time in the 1820s
by the present Carlisle and Stirling road, the toll bar was moved
eastwards to the new crossing. The former toll bar then became
the Old Toll. For generations that name has persisted, applied
to the neighbourhood of the Biggar Road crossing. To the west
the next toll bar was at Coatdyke where a modern building still
bears the name Toll Bar Building. There was no toll bar at the
crossing of Finnie's Lane (Bell Street) which linked the King's
Highway to Cairnhill by a road that crossed the South Burn on
Finnie's Bridge at the foot of Craig Street and followed the line
of our Woodburn Avenue.

Weaving continued to expand. Before 1800 two more
weavers' societies had been founded. At the beginning of the
century the three societies had between them more than 300
members, all adult males; Airdrie's weaving community, men,
women and children, must have formed a substantial part of the
population of 2,745 recorded by the 1801 Census.

By this time the parish school of New Monkland was
inadequate as well as too remote to serve Airdrie's growing

---

*The 'King's Highway' that features in so many of our eighteenth century
feu charters had developed from the road originally made by the monks of
Newbattle to link their eastern and western estates. In terms of modern
streets it is represented by Buchanan Street and Muiryhall Street in
Coatbridge. Keeping to the north of Airdrie South Burn, it passed some 120
yards nearer to Airdrie House than the present road, came on to the line of
Aitchison Street and High Street, turned down South Bridge Street, went
up Hallcraig and Flowerhill Streets and so on to the Colliertree ridge. Its
route from there to Caldercruix is conjectural but we know that it passed
on the north side of Hillend Reservoir and onwards to Bathgate, keeping
all the way on the high ground to the north of the present road. A well-
preserved stretch still exists from Craig Hill to Barbauchlay north of
Armadale.

CIRCUS PROCESSION IN SOUTH BRIDGE STREET
Note the cobbled crossing

needs.   Certainly there were a few small adventure schools in
the town but even they could not accommodate the increasing
numbers desiring education. In 1792 a Chapel of Ease had been
erected in Airdrie — whence the name Chapel Street. Its
committee of management initiated a public subscription for
the building of a school in the town and in 1799 Airdrie Town
School was opened on that very congested site at the foot of
Wellwynd. There a succession of dominies, well-qualified by
the standards of their time, held sway until the school was
closed in 1845.

   In that last decade of the eighteenth century two churches
not of the Establishment appeared, the Reformed Presbyterian
church in the North Loan and the Wellwynd church of the
Associated Synod. The Wellwynd congregation split on one of
the controversial issues of the day and the seceders built them-

JUNCTION OF HALLCRAIG STREET AND BAILLIES LANE
Before 1921

selves a church in Broomknoll. It is a remarkable testimony to the strength of the religious convictions of our forebears that in the course of the next century all three of these congregations built themselves new churches, those that are in use today.

With the opening of the nineteenth century there began a spectacular rise in Airdrie's population from 2,745 in 1801 to 3,474 in 1811 and to 4,862 in 1821. Handloom weaving was still the main industry and the weaving community must have been the greatest contributor to the increase: it is recorded that in the year of Waterloo 1,800 handloom weavers took part in a procession in Airdrie. All of them may not have been resident in the town, for the weavers' societies accepted members from adjoining villages, but credibility is given by the fact that a Government commissioner reported 1,700 hand looms in Airdrie in 1828. As yet no other industry was significant. Certainly mining had not expanded to the same extent as weaving. The only ironworks within five miles was Calder: its three small blast furnaces produced altogether barely 80 tons of iron a week and its requirements of coal and ore could still be satisfied by supplies brought by canal from adjacent pits.

There were no railways, if one excepts the Legbrannock Railway made by Dixon to bring coal to a loading wharf on the

Monkland Canal at Woodhall. Monkland Canal passage boats, introduced in 1813, were in competition with the stage coaches.

Since handloom weaving was essentially a cottage industry, the aspect of Airdrie was more rural than urban and in 1815 an advertisement of Whinhall for sale could claim 'The beauty of the property and the advantages it possesses of communication with Glasgow would make it a very desirable Country Residence'.

So rapid an increase in population entailed much activity in building of houses. There appears to have been little or no regulation of the manner in which they were placed in relation to each other: there was no constituted authority to lay down building lines or to control construction and repair of footpaths and streets other than the King's Highway and the new turnpike road. Only the good sense of the populace preserved tolerable living conditions. But the time had come for such matters to be regulated and in 1821, by a private Act of Parliament, (1 and 2 Geo. IV c.60) Airdrie became a free and independent Burgh of Barony.

THE FIRST FIFTY YEARS

The preamble of the Act opens by asserting that the increase in Airdrie's extent and population had made granting of burghal status 'both expedient and necessary' and ends by defining the extent of the new burgh.

'. . . from and after the passing of this Act the said Town or Village of Airdrie and the Lands adjacent thereto, which are bounded and described as follows: *videlicet*, on the South by the lands of *Gartlee and Rochsolloch;* on the west by the *Linlee Bridge* and the Avenue leading to *Airdrie House*, and a line carried Northward from the centre of the said Avenue; on the North by the lands of *Kypbyre*; and on the East by the *Biggar Road* all the intermediate Lands, Streets, Roads, Lanes and Buildings being included; and also all and whole of the lands called *Well Park, Priestridge Park,* and *Springwells Park,* and *South* and *North Drumbathie Park,* all parts and portions of the Estate of *Rochsolloch and Airdrie,* shall be, and the same are hereby created, united, erected and incorporated into a free and independent Burgh of Barony, to be now and in all Time hereafter called and known by the name of the Burgh of Barony of Airdrie'.

That Airdrie was 'independent' meant that it had, in fact, all the powers of a royal burgh.

The first Town Council was to be elected by and out of those who had contributed not less than two guineas towards the cost of obtaining this private Act of Parliament. In subsequent years the electors were to be those who had contributed not less than three guineas to the Burgh's Common Good Fund. Despite later liberalisation of the franchise, this burgess fee of three guineas continued to be exacted from each newly-elected councillor until the legality of the practice was successfully challenged in 1896.

Those who thus qualified to vote were not necessarily resident in the burgh. Many of them showed little interest in the annual elections: in 1822 only 38 attended the election meeting, in 1823 only 42; that number was almost doubled in 1824 and quadrupled in 1825. In 1829 when 337 voted, no less than 141 of these came from outwith Airdrie, 111 of them from a diversity of places outwith even the parish of New Monkland — Coatbridge, Cumbernauld, Glasgow, Bothwell, Uddingston, Bathgate, Shotts, Wishaw, Omoa, Newarthill, Carluke and Hamilton to name only some; there was even a Thomas But all the way from London.

Although no residential qualification was required of the electors, councillors had to be burgesses who had resided within the limits of the burgh for at least two years prior to the election. Of provost, bailies and treasurer it was further required that they must either possess property within the burgh of the value of not less than £20 sterling annual rent, or occupy a dwelling house within the burgh of annual rent not less than £10. But in the case of the provost these stipulations regarding residence and rental could be dispensed with provided he was a Justice of the Peace for the County of Lanark. Rather surprisingly the Town Clerk, although subject to the jurisdiction of the Town Council, was to be nominated annually by the proprietor *pro tem.* of the estate of Rochsolloch and Airdrie. Even after it became the prerogative of the Town Council, this appointment continued to be made annually until 1913 when Thomas Thomson was appointed the first full-time Town Clerk.

On 28 June 1821, the first election of a Town Council took place; 78 electors attended. On 9 August, the Council got down to business and appointed an assessor, a procurator fiscal, a master of police, a town-crier and officer and a second officer.

It is almost impossible for us to realise the magnitude of the problems that faced our early town councils and the care with which they had to husband their meagre resources. At the end of 1822 the amount of assessment that had been collected was £92-5-7 (£92.28); the balance in the treasurer's hands amounted to £65-18 2½d (65.91) from which the minuscule salaries of the officials had yet to be met as well as the balance of the cost of the Act. (Even so late as 1846 halfpence figured in our municipal accounts). But for the generosity of Miss Margaret Aitchison of Airdrie House, who gave £300 towards the cost of the Act, the burgh would have been burdened with debt. As it was, when the cost of the Act had been cleared, not even a single halfpenny remained in the treasury and the first Town Council had committed their successsors in office to 'repairs on Hallcraig Street, Bell Street, Chapel Street and other places within the burgh'. They had also decided that it was necessary to build a small jail and a Town House. They had, however, had some regard to supplementation of the burgh assessment. In January 1822, they approved a scheme of customs to be levied on all cattle and goods exposed for sale on the streets. The privilege of levying these dues was let annually by public roup until, on 3 May 1894, the Council decided to discontinue these petty customs. And in August 1822, they decided to spend up to three guineas 'on levelling and cleaning part of the quarry for shows and other exhibitions from which a small rent could be drawn'.

Following the second election, George Gentles, 'Town Cryer and Officer', was instructed to get 'a blue coat with a red neck to distinguish him as Criminal Officer for the Burgh'. For a

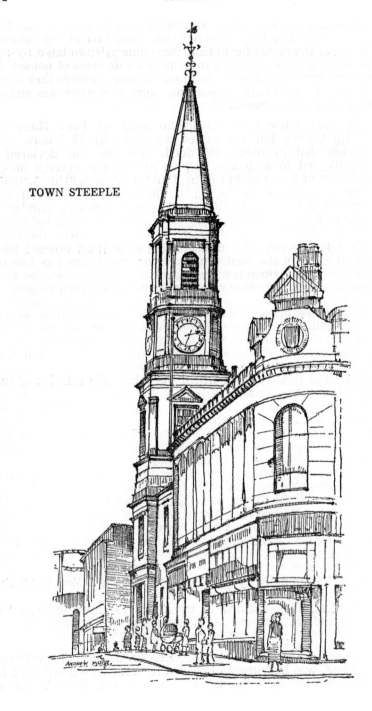

TOWN STEEPLE

generation Geordie's kenspeckle figure was to lead the Council in procession Sunday by Sunday to the Auld Chapel. Speculation on the appearance of the town at this time is stimulated by two other decrees of this Council that 'all seats on sides of houses' be removed within two months and that 'carriers remove their carts from the streets betwixt sunset and sunrise on weekdays and on Sundays during the daytime'.

By 1824 it had been decided to build the Town House on Hallcraig Quarry but vociferous objections by 77 feuars, who contended that in their title deeds this site was declared a commonty, led to a change of plan and it was erected on its present site at a cost of £1,075 by James Orr, 'wright in Airdrie'. For the occasion of the laying of the foundation stone it was ordained that George Gentles should get 'a new coat similar to the one he now has'. Hitherto the only places available for public meetings had been one or other of Airdrie's malt barns, the Town School (after 1799), or the Masons' Hall in High Street (after 1809); until 1826 the annual Town Council election was held in the Masons' Hall. Once completed, the Town House was to have catholicity of use: in the cholera outbreak of 1832 it was pressed into service as an hospital; in 1837 soldiers were quartered in it; for some years the Choral Union was allowed to hold weekly rehearsals there; its use was granted for the lectures of the Airdrie Mechanics' Institution; from 1846 it provided the court-room for the Sheriff-Substitute; in 1854 the Fiscal's room was fitted with shelves to receive the newly-acquired nucleus of our Public Library, the books of the Mechanics' Library; it appears even to have been used on occasion for dancing. What misdemeanours prompted the decision in 1844 that 'the Town House be not let again for dancing'? Fortunately, today, our Town House, save for the copper covering of its steeple, still presents that simple dignified external appearance that was planned by Alexander Baird almost a century and a half ago.

From the beginning streets and footpaths were matters of concern. Systematic naming of streets and numbering of houses began in 1824 and a year later the first Roads Committee was appointed. For road work Statute Labour monies were available: for 1825 these amounted to £118-13/- (£118.65), whilst the burgh assessments came to £114-6-4½d (£114.32), of which, by the way, £44-0-7½d (£44.03) was still outstanding at the end of 1826. Footpaths were the responsibility of property owners who were required to put up kerb stones and lay stone causeways. Some degree of uniformity was insisted upon: in 1843, John Dick, ironfounder, was ordered to remove a cast iron pavement opposite his property in High St. and replace it with stone pavement in the usual way. Another of Dick's innovations that found little favour was a cast iron outside stair at his property in Broomknoll Street. That, too, had to be removed. Extensive and necessary improvements on streets provided relief work for unemployed weavers

OLD HOUSES IN WELLWYND
Before 1925. Note the window shutters.

whose trade had fallen on evil days after a boom period during the Napoleonic wars. In the 1820's the Minutes both of the Town Council and of the Weavers Society have frequent references to the wretchedness of weavers' conditions.

Although the Act of 1821 had given powers to institute street lighting no action appears to have been taken until 1830. Since it was customary then and for many years afterwards to have heavy shutters fitting over the windows of houses there can have been but little light contributed from domestic sources. In 1830 the Airdrie Gas Light Company was incorporated with the Provost and Magistrates as directors *ex officiis,* an arrangement that would be unlikely to meet with approval nowadays. Offers for the erection of street lamps were accepted and in 1831 the Council 'ordained three lamps lighted with oil to be placed at the west end of the old town and three or more as may be found necessary in Hallcraig until such time as the gas pipes can be carried into these streets with advantage'. One lamp was to be erected at 'Mr Finlay's distillery and another one in Chapel Street'. Thus darkness was made visible.

The Scottish Reform Act of 1832 made Airdrie one of the 'parliamentary' burghs. It now combined with Falkirk, Linlithgow, Hamilton and Lanark to return one member to parliament.

Parliamentary franchise became the right of all £10 householders. The burgh was assigned slightly modified and more rational boundaries, the main change being that its eastern boundary became the new Stirling Road instead of the old Biggar Road.

The Council had welcomed the Reform Act but in 1833 it felt impelled to petition Parliament to exclude Airdrie from the provisions of the Bill then under consideration for the reform of local government which included amongst its proposals one to make the local franchise qualification identical with the parliamentary. Reference has already been made to the extraordinary geographical distribution of Airdrie's electorate. The Bill, by introducing a residential qualification, would, it was claimed, reduce Airdrie's electorate from about 500 to about 130: moreover the town would lose all prospects of burgess fees in the future. The Bill, of course, pased to the Statute Book and thereafter the only burgess fees paid were by councillors on their first election and before taking their seats.

The Burgh's first two decades were marked by an extraordinary growth of population: from 4,862 in 1821 it grew to 6,594 in 1831 and to 12,418 in 1841. Over the next three decades only 1,070 were added. It is easy to picture the problems of water supply, of sanitation, of housing and of law and order that arose. Police court fines became a substantial proportion of the town's revenue, from 1845 to 1849 never less than a quarter and on occasion as much as a third. There were many habitual offenders. In 1855 one woman was reported as having 53 previous convictions; her record probably still stands. The accounts for 1841 to 1843 contain such items as 'damage done at (Parliamentary) Election riots', 'Riot expenses and accommodation to the military' and 'Riot assessment'. To strengthen the powers of the magistracy the Airdrie Police Act was obtained in 1849 at a cost of £1,500, equal to a whole year's burgh revenue. In his evidence in support of the Bill Provost James Thomson Rankin stated that in 13 years police court cases had increased fourfold. There was, he claimed, a disproportionate number of 'low beer and spirit shops' and '. . . . upwards of twenty pawnbrokers' shops within the town, all of the lowest and very worst description, their business being the taking in pledge or purchasing for inadequate prices the furniture, wearing apparel and tools of the workmen. Some of these pawnbrokers are also spirit dealers and the wearing apparel and other articles are taken in exchange for intoxicating liquors. The Town Council find these places and the lowest spirit shops to be a very great means of demoralising the working population and a fruitful source of crime and street riots.' A depressing picture indeed but, as we shall see, depicting only one aspect of life in Airdrie at that time.

Water supply must have been a constant worry in those early days. By the 1821 Act the Provost and Magistrates had been empowered to provide suplies by negotiating the purchase of suitable springs or streams and by providing wells fitted with pumps. One such well was provided at Broomknoll in 1826: apparently any surplus from it was conveyed to another well at the foot of Bell Street. At roughly two-yearly intervals three other wells were sunk, one at Burnbrae (hence Pump Lane, now Wilson Street), one on the east side of South Bridge Street and the third at the foot of Hallcraig. In 1845 the Council took over a public well on the lands of Whinhall. A scheme for bringing a piped supply from Tipperdavie spring on the Shotts Hills near Wester Braco proved too expensive for the town's resources. For a short time water was brought in wooden pipes from a spring on Springwells to a well in the town. Public suplies of water, then, were on the most meagre scale. Fortunately many houses had private wells. Municipal responsibility really ended in 1846 when Airdrie and Coatbridge Water Company was formed to construct, in conjunction with the Forth and Clyde Canal Company, the reservoir at Roughrigg that still suplies part of our needs: the Council's statutory powers, however, were not relinquished until the Airdrie Police Act of 1849.

The Town House was only one of a number of public buildings erected in the course of the first fifty years of the burgh. In 1843 a County Prison was built on part of Hallcraig Quarry and in 1849 a J.P. Court House was erected in Callon Street. With growth of population and increase in trade and traffic the practice of exposing goods for sale on stalls in the streets had become a nuisance and so in 1850 the Council provided a market building on another part of the quarry site. This building soon proved inadequate and in 1856 new market buildings replaced the distillery on the gushet between Mill Street and Hallcraig Street. It was becoming increasingly difficult to accommodate Sheriff Court business in the Town House; in 1854 the Council gave the Sheriff notice to quit and when the old market was removed its place was taken by the 'County Buildings' designed to accommodate both Sheriff and J.P. Courts. This building was unique in that it was the only Scottish Sheriff Court building erected and owned by the Commissioners and not by the Crown. On 25 November 1858, within eight months of completion, it was destroyed by fire but was rebuilt and re-opened in June 1859. The year 1856 was also marked by the building by the Monkland Railway Company of a new station in Hallcraig Street to replace one there that had become a byword in the town. An interesting point is that the foundation stones of three buildings, the County Buildings, the Market Buildings, and the new Hallcraig Station, were laid in succession on the same day, 31 July 1856, with full masonic rites.

It may be appropriate at this point to summarise the subsequent history of all of these buildings of which only the Market Buildings remain. The County Prison (the Bridewell) was purchased in 1885 by the Council; it was partly demolished and re-

EXTERIOR OF THE CALLON STREET COURTHOUSE
Demolished about 1962

placed by the Police Court Buildings, opened 12 April 1887.
Callon Street Courthouse ceased to be used as such in 1859. Its
varied uses thereafter have never been fully traced. For a time
in the 1870's it housed a reading room governed by a committee
of its subscribers; from 1878 for some years it was used by the

INTERIOR OF CALLON STREET COURTHOUSE

Airdrie Montrose Lodge of Freemasons; about 1925 it was acquired by the Airdrie branch of the Loyal Order of Ancient Shepherds; latterly it belonged to the Old Age Pensioners' Association. It was demolished about 1962. With passage of time the County Buildings became unsafe; after being propped up for a number of years these were demolished in 1969. Hallcraig Station (Airdrie North) ceased to be used for passengers about 1862 and for goods at the close of 1951. For a time it housed the Mormon Church of the Latter Day Saints. It was demolished in 1966 and its site is now a car park. The Market Buildings were sold in 1899 and converted to a music hall in 1908; cinematographic pictures gradually displaced variety turns and now pictures have given place to bingo.

The last of the public buildings of this period that calls for mention is the Public Hall built near the foot of Hallcraig Street by Airdrie Public Hall Co. Ltd. and opened on 9 April 1867. For some forty years it was the only hall in Airdrie suitable for concerts or larger-scale entertainments. It, too, became a picture house. It was destroyed by fire in April 1953.

Although much housebuilding went on, it was impossible for it to keep pace with the growth of population and many houses took in lodgers; in 1858 no less than 411 houses out of some 1,250 were registered lodging houses. In 1842 the Rev. Daniel Callaghan, Roman Catholic priest at Airdrie, had testified 'many of the houses which receive lodgers have as many as 14 persons in a room'. Comparison of the town plans of 1825 and 1846 with the Ordnance Survey map of 1858 show an interesting pattern of development. The early feuars tended to build their houses on their 'steadings of ground' so that the dwelling house was on or near to the street, and garden ground extended backwards from the house. As the need for houses grew, garden ground was increasingly sacrificed to housing and the maps show the development of closes and courts behind the original building line, such as Miller's Court (now the site of the Sir John Wilson Town Hall) with 26 houses, Main's Court almost directly opposite with 18, and Dick's Court (off Broomknoll Street) with 25. Sometimes this led in course of time to disputes about rights of entry: two notable cases concerned the Mission Hall and Graham Street church; the latter dispute led to the building of South Bridge Street church. Housing density was also increased by replacing single-storey buildings by two-storey. Last century very few Airdrie buildings were higher than this.

MARKET BUILDINGS
Probably about 1911

EXTERIOR OF COUNTY BUILDINGS

SHERIFF COURT HALL
Demolished 1969

The enormous growth of population stemmed not from an inordinately high birth rate but from an influx of residents, some from the Highlands but the vast majority from Ireland Census returns show Irish-born Airdrie residents as 2,093 (17 per cent of total population) in 1841 and 3,095 (23 per cent) in 1851. The increase between 1841 and 1851 is a natural reflection of the increased emigration from Ireland that followed the potato famine of the mid-1840's but the actual numbers are indicative of the change that was coming over the Monklands, the ascendancy of heavy industry over agriculture and handloom weaving. Of the Irish work force in Airdrie in 1841, 31 per cent was engaged in mining and 54 per cent in labouring. Coal and iron industries had shown a rapid expansion from 1828 onwards. In 1801 David Mushet discovered his Blackband Ironstone near Cairnhill and soon had proved it throughout the estate of Airdrie and Rochsolloch. Its successful exploitation in the blast furnace, however, required both Neilson's hot blast and Condie's improved water-cooled tuyere. Once they were available ironworks began to multiply on sites near the Monkland Canal which provided the cheapest and most convenient transport for their products. Much of their ironstone and their coal came from New Monkland, a substantial amount from within the burgh of Airdrie. Bairds of Gartsherrie opened pits at Commonhead, Drumbathie and Rawyards, Neilsons of Summerlee at Broomfield and Chapelside, Wilson of Dundyvan at Chapelside and Millfield (now our Central Public Park). Other pits were at Bellsdyke and Biggar Road. On the verge of the burgh there were pits at Clarkston Drumgelloch and Colliertree. In 1852 the Council were complaining of damage done to Flowerhill and Hallcraig streets by excessive cartage from Baird's Drumbathie ironstone pit. By this time handloom weaving was on the way out. Some weavers found work in the cotton mill that Houldsworth had started in 1832 by the side of the Ballochney Railway; others went into mining. Railways were beginning to be developed in the district. In 1828 the Ballochney Railway had been opened, passing a little to the north of the town. From Leaend, just on the north-west edge of the town a passenger train service to Glasgow was started in 1836: about 1844 or 1845 a branch was brought into Airdrie to a station in Hallcraig Street. Extension of the Ballochney Railway eastwards from Whiterigg to form the Slamannan Railway facilitated the exploitation of the minerals of Slammanan and Muiravonside parishes and brought a whole range of new mining villages within Airdrie's sphere of influence with consequent benefit to her shopkeepers. In 1862 the opening of the Airdrie and Bathgate Junction Railway provided a direct rail link with Edinburgh and the new Airdrie South Station became the starting point for trains to Glasgow.

The expansion of coal and iron industries created a demand for machinery and tools, for boilers and for steam engines both

WORKERS IN AIRDRIE COTTON MILL

stationary and locomotive; foundries expanded and engineering works sprang up. In Bell Street in 1863 Dick and Stevenson began to build locomotives (which were taken down the street to Airdrie South Station under their own steam), steam hammers, pumping engines, winding and other stationary engines and steam navvies. Wellwynd, however, cradled most of the new engineering works. In 1831 David Smith transferred his foundry from Louden Street to part of the old brewery site in Wellwynd; in 1846 he bought the old Town School there and expanded his activities. In 1854 Martin and Stevenson founded Wellwynd Engine Works on part of Smith's site; this works was carried on by various partnerships until 1875 when the firm, by that time Stevenson and Mackay, built larger premises in Chapel Street (Chapel Street Engineering Works) and transferred their activities there. Gibb and Hogg started as engineers alongside them in Wellwynd in 1866 and moved to their large new Victoria Works on Gartlea three years later. All of these moves seem to have been dictated by the need for more space and for railway sidings into the works. Yet another works in Wellwynd was Wellwynd Forge started in 1864 by Sutherland and Shields who came to Airdrie from the Broxburn district, a further testimony to the growing importance of the town. The Standard Works of the

Airdrie Iron Company (now the Burgh Works Department) near the Central Park were founded by J. C. Adamson in 1867. They specialised in plant for gas works and oilworks (of which many had sprung up in New Monkland parish) but also made steam engines of all kinds and various hydraulic machines. All in all, as Airdrie's jubilee year of 1871 approached industrial prospects were rosy.

Provost Rankin in his evidence in support of the Airdrie Police Bill had given a depressing account of his town. But if Airdrie had an inordinate number of pubs and pawnshops, it had also acquired in its first fifty years as a burgh a remarkable collection of religious and social institutions, many of which were active when the Provost made his statement although he chose to remain silent about them. Between 1821 and 1851 no fewer than ten new churches were erected, six of them Presbyterian, one Congregational, one Baptist, one Methodist and one Roman Catholic. In the same period there was a similar proliferation of schools. Two works schools had been established, one in connection with the pits at Gardensquare, the other for the children of workers at the Cotton Mill. Subscription schools had been built at Clarkston and Rawyards and two church schools, the Free West Academy and St. Margaret's Roman Catholic School. St. John's Episcopal School was to follow in 1854. At least ten adventure schools* were competing for pupils in 1841 and in 1849 R. S. C. A. Alexander built Alexander School which was to become Airdrie Academy and then Alexandra School.

Even more surprising was the growth of friendly societies. In 1821 seven had been active; in the next fifty years no less than 28 more were founded in Airdrie, five of them for underground workers, eight yearly societies, and five exclusively Roman Catholic. The interesting point is that all were indigenous: branches of National Orders were not to appear until later in the century. Another, possibly the greatest, local agency for encouraging provident habits was Airdrie Savings Bank founded in 1835.

Two notable philanthropic societies were the New Monkland Orphan Society founded in 1806 and still active in the 1860s and Airdrie Female Benevolent Society (1853) which is still active in its good works.

Among the cultural societies was Airdrie Mechanics Institution and School of Arts founded in 1836 and active until 1892.

All of these activities resulted from an attitude to living that goes far to explain the fact that in 1853, within three months of

*When an optimistic teacher rented a house — or possibly only a room — and set up there as a schoolmaster with no emoluments other than the fees he was able to collect from the pupils whom he was fortunate enough to attract to his school, he was said to be master of an adventure school.

the Public Libraries Act becoming applicable to Scotland, a public meeting of Airdrie electors decided by an overwhelming majority to adopt the Act. They were first in Scotland. Thirteen years were to pass before any other Scottish town followed their example. It is only fair to record that to Provost James Thomson Rankin belongs the honour of having made the first motion to adopt the Public Libraries Act.

Several newspapers were started locally about the middle of the century but only the *Airdrie and Coatbridge Advertiser* has survived. It first appeared on 3 March 1855, published by Archibald Lawson and, until Stamp Duty on newspapers was abolished later that year, was a monthly. The original publishing office was directly opposite the present one from which it was first issued in 1868. For a century now it has been published by Baird and Hamilton, since 1969 a subsidiary of George Outram and Co. Ltd.

About the middle of last century both cricket and football were introduced to Airdrie. At that time cricket appears to have been the more popular. The 'Cricket Club' was allocated ground in Priestrigg Park in 1857 but this official recognition certainly did not mark the beginning of the game in the burgh. In the 1860s at least six cricket clubs were active; two that were still well-known in 1914 failed to survive the first World War and the last cricket pitch within the burgh was lost to Cairnhill housing scheme in 1925. Football under Association rules began, it is claimed, in Airdrie in 1868 although Excelsior, the progenitor of Airdrieonians, was not founded until 1878. Ironically Airdrie Cricket Club gave a fillip to the rival game by instituting the Airdrie Charity Cup in 1884. This cup is preserved in the Airdrie Museum.

In 1870 the last Airdrie Race Meeting was held. It has been recorded that after the opening of the new Glasgow–Airdrie–Bathgate road in 1795 the Airdrie Lammas Fair came to be known as the Lammas Race Fair since it had become customary to hold both horse and foot races on that day on the stretch of the road between Airdrie House gate and Drumgelloch. In the early years this diversion may not have been objectionable but on 7 August 1845—significantly just after a Lammas Fair—the Town Council resolved 'to prevent all foot or other races within the limits of the burgh in time coming' and instructed the magistrates 'to issue proclamations and carry the resolution into effect'. The Council may not have had in mind a literal interpretation of their edict; however, on 5 September 1850, a race meeting was held on a field at Thrashbush outwith the burgh bounds. In 1851 a field on Drumbathie Farm, between Bore Road and Motherwell Road, was leased for conversion into a racecourse. Thus Airdrie Race Meeting came into being. On the expiry of the lease in 1870 a renewal was refused and all the buildings had to be removed.

The grandstand was bought by Provost Adam; from its ashlar work he built his house in Victoria Place. There is some evidence that the track of the old racecourse was later used for trotting races. Under certain lighting conditions parts of the outline of the track are still discernible.

In 1877 the old racecourse became the golf course of the newly-formed Airdrie Golf Club (who removed to Rochsoles in 1884) and it was the venue of Airdrie Highland Games before these were transferred to Broomfield Park. Now the recently-revived Games are held on Rawyards Park on the opposite side of the South Burn from the old racecourse.

MARKET STREET ABOUT 1925

THE SECOND FIFTY YEARS

The period 1871–1921 saw the first substantial extension of the burgh beyond its original boundaries. Contemporaneously with the uniting of Whifflet, Dundyvan, Langloan, Gartsherrie, Coatbridge and part of Coatdyke into the new burgh of Coatbridge, Airdrie annexed the eastern part of Coatdyke (including Rochsolloch Ironworks), the eastern part of Rawyards and the villages of Clarkston, Drumgelloch and Colliertree, altogether an area of 387 acres with a population of 3,126. Apart from this accession the rate of growth of Airdrie's population had begun to level off and from 1871 to 1921 it increased only from 13,488 to 25,093.

A changing pattern in administration was emerging. In 1889 Lanarkshire County Council was created and little by little this larger administrative unit began to erode the prerogatives of the Town Council and of other locally-elected bodies. In 1918 Airdrie ceased to be one of the 'Falkirk Burghs' and was united with Coatbridge in the Coatbridge Division of Lanarkshire to return one member to Parliament. The undemocratic Parochial Board that had held sway for almost half a century was replaced in 1895 by an elected Parish Council. Water supply that had been in the hands of a private supply company became in 1903 the responsibility of Airdrie, Coatbridge and District Water Trust. Gas supply became a municipal undertaking in 1904.

Education had long since become a problem quite beyond the resources of the Kirk Session of New Monkland and within that parish three school boards were established in 1873, Airdrie School Board to organise education within the burgh as then defined, Clarkston and New Monkland to be responsible between them for the non-burghal areas of the parish. Despite subsequent changes in Airdrie's boundaries, the spheres of influence of these three school boards were never re-defined.

The problems facing Airdrie School Board were *mutatis mutandis* very much those that from time to time have beset their successors. Existing schools were grossly overcrowded even by the standards of the day: Graham Street School (long known as the Penny School and now a discotheque) had 240 pupils; St. John's Episcopal School (in the building now the Girl Guides Hall) had 202; a small school in Hallcraig Street with only 484 square feet of floor area had 150. Altogether, it was calculated, the existing schools had air and floor space for only 1,474 children

PERFORMING BEAR IN GRAHAM STREET

The picture is dated as before 1904 by the absence of tram rails and by the E.U. Congregational Church where the Masonic Temple now stands.

yet 2,575 were in attendance; a further 861 between 5 and 13 years of age were not attending any school. For a temporary alleviation of the position the Board rented the Mission Hall in High Street and the ground floor of the Methodist Church in Bell Street. Plans were commissioned for the building of Victoria and Albert Schools (each to provide 400 places) and for an extension to Rawyards School for 150 pupils. Victoria School was opened on 1 February 1876, and Albert on 7 August of the same year. Chapelside followed on 5 November 1883; three days earlier Rawyards School had been closed. Fees continued to be charged in all schools—the aim being to make each school as far as possible self-supporting—until in 1886 the Board decided to discontinue fees in all their evening schools. Three years later, in accordance with the 1889 Act, they ceased to exact fees from pupils in the infant classes and in Standards I to V in Albert, Chapelside and Victoria Schools, continuing however to charge 4d a week in Standards VI and Ex-VI. In Airdrie Academy fees continued to be charged throughout the school, Infants 1d a week, Standards I to IV 2d a week, and Standards V, VI and Ex-VI 4d a week. From time to time all of the schools had be extended and in 1901 Rochsolloch School was built to serve the Coatdyke end of the town. A new Airdrie Academy (secondary) was built in 1895 (whereupon the old building was renamed Alexandra School) and a successor alongside it in 1908. Two schools continued as independent undertakings, the Free West Academy until 1885 and St. John's Episcopal School until 1884. All school boards were dissolved in 1919 when the newly-constituted Lanarkshire Education Authority took over responsibility for education throughout Lanarkshire.

It has already been mentioned that the Public Library was first accommodated in the Town House. From 1860 it flitted to and fro between rented premises—the new Market Buildings from 1860 to 1877 and again 1885 to 1894 and a hall on the first floor of premises on the west side of Bank Street from 1877 to 1885— until, thanks to supplementation of local subscriptions by Andrew Carnegie, it became possible to erect in Anderson Street a library building, opened 3 August 1894, which also provided a reading room; on the upper floor a museum was opened in 1895; and in 1896 an observatory was added on the roof. By 1911 this library building was already too small for the demands made upon it. In 1913 Andrew Carnegie promised a substantial grant towards the cost of a new building but the first World War put the scheme out of mind until the early 1920s.

Despite the many schisms and unions of the nineteenth century the Church continued to grow and prosper in Airdrie. Between 1875 and 1904 eight new church buildings appeared, four of them new buildings for existing congregations (one Presbyterian, one Baptist and two Congregational), the others for new congregations (Presbyterian, Congregational, Episcopal and Roman Catholic). Thirty-five years passed before any more new churches were built.

At quite an early date the Council had realised the desirability of providing spaces for open-air recreations and in 1856 they had leased part of Priestrigg Park for use as a 'public green or recreation ground'. The first Airdrie Academy stood on another part of this park which before long became known as Academy Park. In 1886 Mr Alexander made a gift of the park to the town; ten years later he offered Millfield Park in exchange provided the town renounced all claim to Academy Park. Millfield Park, originally the mill lands of Airdrie Grain Mill, was more central and by purchasing the land between it and Bore Road the Council brought into being our Central Park. This happened on the eve of Sir John Wilson's purchase of the Airdrie estate and on entering into possession he made a gift of £1,000 towards the cost of laying out the park, the first of his many benefactions to the town. Central Park was opened on 19 November 1897. Between 1909 and 1913, by culverting the South Burn at the west end of the town and filling in the ravine between Alexander Street and the railway, the West End Park was constructed. Again Sir John Wilson met the cost of laying out the paths and flower plots. Centenary Park, on the opposite side of Alexander Street, was completed in 1921, the burgh's centenary year.

In 1896 the burgh obtained powers to provide electric tram-ways. These powers were transferred to the British Electric Tramways Company and on 6 February 1904, a tramway was opened for traffic from Carlisle Road (the 'Terminus') to the west end of Coatbridge at Woodside Street or, as the tram indicator boards more appropriately had it, Millbrae. It was a single track with passing places. Airdrie and Coatbridge jointly acquired the undertaking in 1920 and sold it two years later to Glasgow Corporation. The last tram ran on 4 November 1956.

A Provisional Order for supply of electricity, obtained in 1897, was ultimately assigned to the Scottish House-to-House Electricity Company and in 1902 part of the burgh was lit by 16 candle power electric lamps supplemented by a few arc lamps about the centre of the town.

Between 1881 and 1911 housebuilding appears to have kept pace with the growth in population and the average density of population remained pretty constant at five persons per house. Sewerage arrangements, however, had fallen behind. Except through the very centre of the town the South Burn lay open; there was even less culverting of the North Burn and in the 1890s these burns and their tributaries received all the town's sewage and fed it into the Luggie and ultimately the North Calder. Coatbridge sewage also went into the Luggie and the County authorities complained that the character of the North Calder had been completely altered right down to its junction with the Clyde. Legal action against the two town councils was repeatedly threatened. In 1890, some sort of general drainage scheme for Airdrie was begun and at that time the responsibilities of Sanitary Inspector were transferred from the Chief Constable to the Burgh Surveyor. This drainage scheme did little more than enclose most of the smaller open sewers; no provision was made for treat-ment of sewage and the condition of the North and South Burns was so bad in 1900 that the Council were ordered to have them flushed periodically with fresh water. Even so late as 1904 citizens were protesting about the sewage that entered the pond in Central Park. Steps were taken to remedy these local causes for complaint but it was 1919 before construction of a main sewer system was begun and 1928 before sewage purification works were in operation. The South Burn continued to be used as a sewer until 1926.

Until the first World War many tenement properties still had dry closets and associated middens. From 1853 contractors had been employed for cleansing purposes but in 1897 the burgh set up its own cleansing department using part of the Market Buildings and stables. In 1902 Wester Craigneuk Farm was leased for disposal of refuse: it was purchased in 1932 and is now the site of Craigneuk housing scheme. The post of Sanitary Inspector became a separate appointment in 1903.

AIRDRIE HOUSE

Demolished 1964

Airdrie's first hospital built as such was the small fever hospital erected in Wilson Street in 1871 after the Bairds of Gartsherrie had declined to allow the grandstand of Airdrie Race Course to be leased for that purpose. The Wilson Street hospital continued in service until 1927 when it was replaced by Wester Moffat Hospital. Airdrie House Maternity Hospital, serving both Airdrie and Coatbridge, was opened on 10 August, 1919.

Only our more elderly residenters can recall the nature of our streets before the substitution of "tarmac" for ordinary "metal". Ordinary macadamised or "metalled" roads were laid with pieces of whinstone of roughly cubic shape of a size that would pass through a two-inch ring. Here and there there were stone magazines—rectangular bays walled on three sides—in which were deposited stocks of whin for road works; occasionally men could be seen busy with knapping hammers breaking stones to this size that John Loudon McAdam had decreed was best. However well compacted the surface of a metalled road might have been to begin with, passage of traffic raised a lot of dust which in wet weather produced an incredible amount of mud. In summer weather attempts were made to keep the dust under control by spraying water from a horse-drawn watering cart that was usually accompanied by a retinue of barefoot boys. The mud was even worse than the dust. At some important crossings whinstone cobbles were laid from which mud could fairly easily be brushed. From the rest of the roadway mud was removed periodically by hand-drawn scrapers that drew it towards the gutter. Until this mud was carted away the unwary could easily step off the pavement into several inches of mud. The dust nuisance worsened as motor vehicles multiplied and became a potent discouragement to cyclists. It is amusing to reflect that motors which at first drove cyclists off the roads later brought them back in increasing numbers once the motorists had successfully agitated for tarmac roads. Tarmac began to be laid in Airdrie in 1914–15.

The Caledonian Railway opened a branch line from Langloan into Airdrie in 1886, providing an independent link with Glasgow (Central Low Level Station). Their Airdrie terminus occupied the grounds of Broomfield House. Two years later they opened their branch line from Airdrie to Newhouse. It had been intended to carry this branch on to Omoa where it would have joined the Caledonian line to Edinburgh; in 1901 the Town Council agreed to press the railway company to complete their line to Omoa but nothing came of their representations nor of pressure some years later by our local Merchants' Association.

In the course of the burgh's second half-century its industries had many ups and downs. Old-established firms closed down but new industries appeared and on balance prospects seemed bright.

Dick and Stevenson were the first to go. In 1890 their last two pugs were driven down Bell Street to Airdrie South Station; the firm and its associated New Monkland Forge Company were wound up and "Jumbo", the forge company's steam hammer in their Craig Street works, ceased to deave residents in the western part of the town. Engineering in Bell Street had come to an end and some 140 men were thrown out of work.

Some expansion took place in Smith's works in Wellwynd but naturally the greatest developments were on sites that could have railway sidings such as Chapel Street and Bellsdyke.

Off Chapel Street Martyn Brothers started an iron foundry in 1875. About the same time Stevenson and Mackay built on an adjoining site the new and larger works to which they removed from Wellwynd. Their old works was absorbed into Smith's establishment. On a site between Martyn's foundry and Chapel Street Shiels and McNichol, boilermakers, began business in 1885. Following the death of Robert Stevenson in 1892, Stevenson and Mackay's engineering works were acquired by Mackay, Main and Dunn. When they gave up business in the following year their works were taken over by the Weldless Steel Chain Syndicate Ltd., a company formed to exploit Graham Stevenson's patents. After their failure in 1896 the works were bought by John Martyn (of Martyn Brothers) who let them for about three years to the Delta Metal Company of London. The Martyn Tempered Grit Co. Ltd. took over the works in 1910. This may seem a surprising variety of activity concentrated in so small an

area but it was to be surpassed by developments in the Bellsdyke
area south of Hogg Street and straddling the Caledonian railway
line. Gibb and Hogg it will be remembered were already
established on the north side of that street.

First in the field on the lands of Bellsdyke were Inglis and
Hossack with their Albert Engineering Works in 1885, a year
before the Caledonian branch line was opened. Nine years later
the firm became G. Inglis and Co. Ltd. There followed two small
shortlived foundry firms, the Alert Foundry (1899-1904) and
Airdrie Steel Foundry Ltd. (1899-1903). The buildings of the
Alert Foundry were taken over and enlarged in 1905 by John
Napier, Son and Co. who renamed them the Empire Works; they
introduced the casting of domestic grates, a trade they had carried
on in Kirkintilloch for the preceding thirty years. In 1904 the
steel foundry was acquired and renamed Bellsdyke Works by
John Spence and Sons, a plumbing firm founded in 1835 who
were also brassfounders. On the opposite side of Bellsdyke Road
from Inglis's works the Caledonian Wire Rope Works were
erected in 1898. Then in 1901 the North West Rivet, Bolt and
Nut Factory went into production on the opposite side of the
Caledonian railway from Inglis's works and adjacent to the Alert
Foundry and the Steel Foundry. In the same quarter of the town
alongside Gibb and Hogg's works a grit works was started in
1900 by William McGregor. From the same site two other firms
concerned with the manufacture and grading of abrasives carried
on their operations, the Diamond Steel Manufacturing Co. Ltd.
(1905) and Corundum Ltd. (1909). McGregor was a director of
each of them.

Near the west end of the burgh A. and J. Stewart and Menzies
Ltd. built in 1898-1900 their Imperial and Climax tube works.
In 1903 the firm merged with Lloyd and Lloyd Ltd. to form
Stewarts and Lloyds Ltd. Adjacent to Rochsolloch Ironworks an
iron foundry was started by Smith and Hamilton about 1888.
Towards the east end of the town in 1900 another foundry and
engineering works was built by Dunwoodie Brothers who called it
the Carlisle Works. It stood on the east side of Carlisle Road and
just south of the Airdrie-Bathgate railway, then the burgh
boundary in that region. Dunwoodie's venture was unfortunate
and in 1902 the site was taken over by Finlay Finlayson and
became the Atlas Works; since then the site has been continuously
in use as a scrap yard and steel stockyard. Also in 1900 near
Clarkston Station, again just outwith the burgh boundary, Caldervale Forge began the manufacture of spades and shovels. It has
now diversified its activities: shovelmaking has declined but this
is now the only firm in Lanarkshire making any shovels at all.

One may well ask what brought these new industries to
Airdrie. Undoubtedly availability of sites and accessibility of
raw materials must have weighed heavily in the decisions.
Coatbridge was the principal iron-producing district in Scotland

IRON SHINGLERS IN THE CENTENARY PROCESSION
Note the protective clothing

but in Coatbridge sites were at a premium: when David Colville ended his partnership with Thomas Gray in Clifton Works in 1869 he could find no suitable site in Coatbridge for his new works. Another factor must have been the existence in Airdrie of a growing pool of traditionally skilled workmen. And, not least, Airdrie's rates were low.

At the beginning of the twentieth century, then, Airdrie had the Airdrie Iron Co., Gibb and Hogg and G. Inglis and Co. (each employing about 150) together with Martyn Brothers (employing about 50) all engaged in heavier engineering activities, building pugs, stationary steam engines of all kinds, steam hammers and both land and marine boilers. The other foundries and smaller engineering works employed, it was estimated, about 200 altogether. So about 700 found employment in engineering. The wire rope works employed about 150, the bolt works about 400 and the tube works before long almost 1,000. Airdrie Cotton Mill provided work for nearly 1,000, most of them women. In addition many found work in the vicinity of Airdrie in the iron and tube works of Coatbridge and in Calderbank steelworks, which seemed by 1901 under James Dunlop and Co. Ltd. to have reached stability after a chequered history extending over the

GIBB & HOGG'S ERECTING SHOP

The work in progress is a pair of 42 inch coupled winding engines
for a Yorkshire colliery.

preceding half-century. The paper mills at Moffat Mills and
Caldercruix had been extended and rag-sorting at Caldercruix
employed so many women that for many years a special mill-
workers' train was run to take them to and from their work.
Within the burgh a number of women were engaged in small
hosiery factories. These factories were in the main shortlived.
The buildings of three remain: the Craig Street Victoria Hosiery
Mills (1897) of the Airdrie Hosiery Company, after being in turn
the Territorials' Drill Hall and the premises of a motor engineer
and mill furnisher, have been since 1947 Messrs. Kidds'
confectionery works; Brown's hosiery factory (1915) in Chapel
Street now forms part of the ironmongery shop of Henry Scott
and Son; and in Graham Street McGibbon's factory after housing
an amazing variety of activities (a private school, Airdrie Service
Club, the Apostolic Church, the Knights of Israel, a Temperance
Reform Association, a Spiritualist Church, and the Friends of the
Soviet Union) seems to have settled down to more permanent use
as a restaurant.

Many casual workers were brought to the district by the
upsurge in local industry around 1900. By that time the number
of lodging houses in Airdrie appears to have dwindled to two,
one in Wellwynd and one in Bell Street, and the Airdrie Model

Lodging House Co. Ltd. was formed. This company built two 'models', one in Gartlea in 1900 the other in Rochsolloch Road in the following year. The building of the latter still stands but is now a hosiery factory. Gartlea 'model' was demolished about 1917.

The mood of optimism with which the twentieth century opened was soon dispelled. In 1911 Gibb and Hogg Ltd. resolved on liquidation. A year later the Airdrie Iron Co. Ltd. followed suit. Their decisions appear to have been dictated by purely personal considerations; there is no evidence that either firm was in any real financial trouble. As we have seen, the small firms that went out of business between 1900 and 1905 after brief lives had all been replaced. Not so with these two major firms. Some 300 jobs were lost, apparently irretrievably for both works were stripped of plant and machinery. The Airdrie Iron Company's Standard Works lay empty until taken over by the Burgh Works Department in 1930. In 1912 part of Gibb and Hogg's site became a showground and in 1913 their iron foundry was acquired by Robert Maitland, who had been in business as a founder since 1901 in part of Dick and Stevenson's old works in Bell Street. Most of the rest of the site was taken over in 1916 by Beardmore who set up two very large steam hammers for forging work and went on to erect a large machine shop that was almost ready for work when the Armistice was signed. Its gas furnaces were never connected to the mains. The eastmost bay of this shop was built over the site of the model lodging house. Both bays have now been converted into Baxter's bus garage.

Two early twentieth century events that have had far-reaching social consequences were the coming of the cinema and the introduction of motor buses.

It has already been mentioned that the Town Council sold the Market Buildings in 1899. The new owners continued to let the stalls and stances until they converted the market hall about 1908 into a variety theatre, the Hippodrome, in which Bioscope pictures also were shown. In 1911 it underwent considerable reconstruction: its walls were raised four feet; a new steel roof was put on; the old front shops were removed and in the hall itself a sloping floor was installed. The prices of admission were 2d, 4d and 6d. The most expensive seats were at the very front, a reflection of the importance of variety in the Hippodrome's programmes. Variety continued longer in the Hippodrome than in any other place of entertainment in Airdrie. And as late as 1917 it had a week of opera provided by the John Ridding English Opera Company, when prices (including War Tax) were 7d and 1s 2d with booked seats at 1s 6d.

The Public Hall was the venue for the concerts of local choirs and bands as well as the many meetings and musical entertainments organised by the local lodge of Good Templars. Like the

Hippodrome the Public Hall began to stage variety shows and exhibit the Bioscope. A typical advertisement in April 1907, offered 'Sydney Prince with 40 miles of talking pictures' which included Oliver Twist in 12 scenes and 'The curfew shall not ring tonight' in 24 scenes. But already in February 1907, the I.O.G.T. had organised a 'cinematograph display' by Gardner and Company of Glasgow. (Five years earlier Lizars of Glasgow had given in Coatbridge Town Hall what appears to have been the first demonstration of the cinematograph in the Monklands.) By 1911 the Public Hall was featuring B.B. ('Bright and Beautiful — name registered and protected') cinematographic pictures. Like the Hippodrome it had a face lift in 1911. Electric light was installed. We are told that the arched ceiling was painted ivory white, the walls turquoise blue and the proscenium green and gold. Care was taken to preserve the portraits of poets and dramatists in the panels around the front of the gallery.

In 1911 the Pavilion in Graham Street came into being. The fashionable craze for roller skating struck Airdrie about 1908-9 when sessions of roller skating were run in the Albion Hall (the original Baptist Church) in Graham Street. The popularity of these induced the Dunsmores to build a large roller skating rink north of Broomfield Park. Two years later the craze had passed and the skating rink underwent internal reconstruction to become the Pavilion, a music hall which also showed the new cinematographic pictures. At its opening on 23 October 1911, the variety programme was supplemented by a film of Rob Roy made at Aberfoyle and starring the famous Durward Lely as Frances Osbaldistone. Seats downstairs were priced as in the Hippodrome but in the balcony one could be a real toff and have a reserved tip-up chair for a shilling. The original Pavilion was a corrugated iron structure. It was completely destroyed by fire in 1917; the better-known brick building was erected in 1919. It was closed in 1970 to allow redevelopment of the site.

The last cinema to appear in Airdrie—the only one to be built as a cinema and now the only remaining one—was the New Cinema in Broomknoll Street opened in February, 1920.

Undoubtedly Airdrie lacked a hall suitable for larger public and social functions. For many functions the Public Hall was too small and it could not always be available for those who wished to use it. In 1910 the Council had before them a proposal that the municipality should erect a Town Hall of suitable dimensions. On this issue the ratepayers were divided and the Council were on the point of taking a plebiscite when Sir John Wilson came forward with an offer of £10,000 towards the cost. In the end he defrayed the whole cost, some £13,500. The Sir John Wilson Town Hall, opened on 16 October 1912, was built on the site of the noisome Miller's Court to the plans of James Thomson, an Airdrie architect. He, however, bears no responsibility for the present tasteless decor.

MILLER'S COURT
Now the site of the Sir John Wilson Town Hall

SIR JOHN WILSON TOWN HALL

At the beginning of the twentieth century horse brakes provided somewhat infrequent services from Airdrie to villages, such as Greengairs, that had no rail services and, in competition with the railway, to Caldercruix and Coatbridge. On 18 September 1905, a motor car service to Greengairs was started. In 1912 the tramway company began to run motor buses to Caldercruix; these were taken over in 1914 by Scottish General Transport. The first World War restricted development but soon after it ended motor services by cars and buses multiplied and on some routes there were dangerous rivalries reminiscent of the stage coaches.

When, under the National Insurance Act of 1911, the State first embarked upon social insurance, the impact on our friendly societies was less than might have been expected. Between 1871 and 1921 some sixteen branches of National Orders—such as the United Order of Mechanics, the Shepherds, the Rechabites, the Foresters, the Oddfellows, the Sons of Temperance, the Good Templars—were formed in the burgh, as well as four purely local societies with no extra-mural affiliations. Over the same period twelve Airdrie societies were dissolved, seven of them after the 1911 Act, but surprisingly our yearly dividing societies were not adversely affected: in 1921 the five remaining yearly societies had a combined membership of 6,700, eighty per cent. more than the six societies of 1911, although over that decade the population of the burgh had increased by less than three per cent.

Mention of Rechabites, Sons of Temperance and Good Templars recalls that in this period of Airdrie's history the 'Temperance Movement' was militant. The Airdrie lodge of the I.O.G.T. became, with 3,750 members, the largest in the world. Outwith their propaganda work its members were active in promoting weekly, sometimes twice-weekly, concerts and entertainments; for many years they ran a male voice choir and a football team; and for more than 25 years they produced an annual kinderspiel which became a pantomime after things Teutonic were viewed with disfavour. At every opportunity they pressed for a reduction in the number of public houses; their efforts resulted in a reduction from one for every 160 inhabitants in 1891 to one for every 1,030 in 1950.

When war was declared in 1914 our local Territorials were immediately mobilised. Airdrie had had almost a century of civilian training for military service, first through the Militia and Yeomanry and later through the Volunteers and Territorials. The local Volunteers, founded in 1859, were disbanded in 1897 despite a storm of justified public protest. From 1885 their drill hall had been in Chapel Street in what is now the Girl Guides Hall. It was, of course, the Volunteers' rifle range on Gartlea that gave the 'Targets' their name; the new range at Plains came into use in the 1880s. In 1903 the Second Lanarkshire Royal Engineers were recruited. For their local drill hall they rented the disused hosiery factory in Craig Street (since 1947 a confectionery works) until in late 1909 or early 1910 a drill hall was built beside Coatdyke railway station. Airdrie and Coatbridge Territorials formed the first Territorial Field Company to land in France and in the course of the war they created an army record for the number of decorations won by officers and men of a field company. A large number of Airdrieonians served in other branches of H.M. Forces and Airdrie suffered the grievous loss of over 450 men killed.

The war, of course, put a stop to house building. In fact, from about 1911 few houses had been built for letting. The Housing Act of 1919 empowered the Town Council to make good this deficiency in some limited measure and they were not slow to act. Building of Council houses was begun at Drumbathie, at Clarkston and at the west end of Aitchison Street. In each of these schemes some houses were occupied by the end of 1920. But between 1911 and 1921 the number of houses in the burgh had increased only from 4,873 to 5,067.

Celebration of the Armistice and of the end of the war seemed to run on with little breathing space into the celebrations that marked the centenary of the erection of Airdrie into a burgh. Because of the miners' strike these celebrations had to be postponed for three months; the official proceedings started on Thursday 22 September 1921, and extended until Tuesday, 27 September. On Thursday boxes each containing a pound of tea were presented to 500 'deserving poor people'. Next day the school children of the burgh (some 6,000 in all) were treated to special entertainments in three of Airdrie's cinemas, the New Cinema, the Pavilion and the Hippodrome. In the evening 165 guests attended a dinner in the Sir John Wilson Town Hall at which Sir James Knox was the principal speaker. A sports meeting in Broomfield Park on the Saturday morning was followed in the afternoon by a spectacular procession through the main streets in which nine bands and forty units representative of the various activities and interests in the burgh took part. This procession was headed by mounted police followed by the local Territorials. Then came the Provost, Magistrates and Town Councillors in carriages, with immediately behind them the local youth organisations—Stewarts and Lloyds Cadet Corps, the Boy Scouts, Boys Brigade, Girl Guides and Brownies. The next eight units comprised friendly and temperance societies with pride of place given to Airdrie Weavers Society (then aproaching its ter-jubilee) followed by the Free Gardeners, the Ancient Order of Shepherds, the Orange Lodges, the Good Templars, the Sons of Temperance, the Rechabites, the Ancient Order of Hibernians and the Irish National Foresters. The bulk of the rest of the procession represented the various industries and the rear was brought up by Airdrie's three Masonic Lodges.

This procession was marshalled at the west end of Aitchison Street facing westwards and moved off at 1.30 p.m. to traverse

the town eastwards from Alexander Street to the car terminus
thence northwards to Rawyards Cross, westwards to South Bridge
Street and southwards to Bank Street.   There the Territorials
divided to line both sides of the street; the Provost and his
entourage mounted a platform in front of the Town House and
the Provost took the salute of each unit as it passed.   After dusk
there was a fireworks display in Broomfield Park.   A special
centenary service followed on Sunday 25th September in the
West Parish Church and as the final act in the celebrations an
entertainment was given on the following Tuesday to the residents
of Thrashbush Home.

A cine film of the celebrations was shown in local cinemas.
If a copy still exists it would certainly make interesting viewing
now.   One permanent record that resulted was, of course, Sir
John Knox's book *'Airdrie, a Historical Sketch'* based on the
collection of records of Airdrie's history and traditions that had
been made by Sir James and before him by his uncle, whose
work in this connection has never been properly acknowledged.

THE GUSHET HOUSE
Demolished 1937

THE THIRD FIFTY YEARS

The 1920s and 1930s were to prove testing times for Airdrie. In the recession that followed the war years her industries were hard hit and many families emigrated. In consequence of this and of the severity of war casualties the increase in population in the intercensal period 1921-31 was very small, only from 25,093 to 25,954; and 366 out of this increase of 861 were accounted for by the population taken over when the burgh was extended in 1927.

When peace came the Beardmore works in Airdrie ceased to function. Then in 1923 the cotton mill closed down and later was sold for demolition. The engineering firm of G. Inglis and Co. Ltd. went into liquidation in 1928 and their successors of the same name, later changed to Inglis, Arnott and Co. Ltd. survived only until 1931. In 1928, too, the Caledonian Wire Rope Works were closed following their purchase by British Ropes Ltd. Three years later the extensive saw mills of William Shanks and Sons off Chapel Street passed out of existence. Corundum Ltd. had gone into liquidation in 1926 and when the Diamond Steel Manufacturing Co. Ltd. followed in 1933 the grit works in Gartlea Road came to an end. All these works were within the burgh. Outwith the burgh other closures were taking place. Calderbank Steelworks were closed in 1929 when the new firm Colvilles Ltd. merged the interests of David Colville and Sons Ltd. with those of James Dunlop and Co. Ltd. Soon afterwards the Calderbank site was cleared and it has never been used since. Iron and steel works in Coatbridge were also hard hit: the blast furnaces at Gartsherrie were blown out in March 1925 for the first time since 1829; those at Calder and Carnbroe were never re-lit after the miners' strike in 1921 and Summerlee closed in 1930. Some of the tube works were scrapped. Any works that remained in Airdrie or Coatbridge found orders hard to get and prices unprofitable.

In the general depression few industries were forthcoming to replace those lost and broadly speaking the contribution of the newcomers to the problem of unemployment was slender. In 1926 the Grit Company of Scotland Ltd. took over the Lion Foundry in Rochsolloch Road (formerly the iron foundry of Smith and Hamilton) and carried on the manufacture of steel grit there until 1968. Aerocrete (Scotland) Ltd. occupied Beardmore's factory in Gartlea Road from 1932 until 1942 for making concrete building blocks. A local firm of wholesale fruit merchants (Marshalls) adapted the former wire rope works for the growing of mushrooms, a venture that was not very successful; then in 1938 the buildings were taken over by Crimpy Crisps Ltd. who made potato crisps there until fire destroyed their factory in 1969. The buildings of Inglis's Albert Works were bought in 1934 by the Springbank Tile Co. Ltd. but this was merely a removal into the burgh of a firm already established on the outskirts.

It is impossible for anyone who did not live through these times even to imagine what they were like. In 1931 Airdrie Labour Exchange reported that 50 per cent of the registered insured population were unemployed; by 1937 trade prospects had improved somewhat but still 43.9 per cent were totally unemployed. In this appalling state of affairs Airdrie Churches Council made a valiant effort to counter the demoralising hopelessness that springs from protracted unemployment. The ministers of the town, together with a number of public-spirited laymen, established in 1931 a Mutual Service Club which met initially in Airdrie Evangelistic Association's Wilson Memorial Hall in Hallcraig Street. Classes were organised in such practical subjects as joinery, boot repairing and radio construction. The Education Committee lent support by providing instruction in more academic subjects. Classes in physical training were also available and camp holidays for families were organised. But in 1935 notice was given that after the following year the Hall would not be available to the Club. This social experiment, however, had attracted national interest and a building in Graham Street, specially designed for the activities of the Mutual Service Club, was provided by the Scottish Council for Social Service and was formally opened on 12 October 1936. In its first session in its own premises the Club had 633 members. This is the building that is now the Community Centre.

The Town Council set up a New Industries Committee entrusted with the task of endeavouring to attract new industries to Airdrie but in face of the general depression it had not achieved much up to the outbreak of war in 1939. The establishment of Chapelhall Industrial Estate earlier that year caused hopes to rise in the district but although a variety of types of employment became available these required more women than men. During the second World War there was not a significant increase in the number of jobs available in Airdrie itself. Even after the war no substantial improvement in the situation was apparent until in 1949 two large factories were attracted to Airdrie, Boots Pure Drug Co. Ltd. to Rawyards, and Banner Textiles Ltd. to Rochsolloch. Between them they employ about 1,200, the majority of them women. Airdrie Electronics Ltd., later renamed Pye Scottish Telecommunications Ltd., came to Airdrie in 1958 and have expanded until now they employ over 1,000 workers in the manufacture of telephones and a wide variety of electronic equipment. Outwith the burgh the various firms on Newhouse Industrial Estate (1948) have provided a very large number of jobs for Airdrieonians. There has been in the past a feeling of uncertainty about these two local industrial estates since some firms turned out to be birds of passage. It is true, however, to say that no factory has remained for long without a tenant; and employees have shown a capacity for adaptation to new skills.

In the early 1960s the number of unemployed began to rise again to a degree that caused concern. Moffat Paper Mill was closed in 1963 and two years passed before it was acquired by Inver House Distillers for conversion to a distillery. The North West Rivet Bolt and Nut Factory had been bought over by Guest, Keen and Nettlefold and was closed in 1966, perhaps a natural consequence of the introduction of the new techniques of welding which was replacing rivetting in shipbuilding. In the Coatbridge area Rochsolloch, Northburn, Waverley and Coats Works were all scrapped as was Gartsherrie Works that had been modernised only a few years earlier.

However in 1969 Ronald Lyon Estates Ltd. began to build an industrial estate within Airdrie on a site bordered by Carlisle Road and Brownsburn Road. The first factory was taken by Hoover Ltd. for the manufacture of fractional horsepower motors. It has just been announced that the old-established Airdrie printers John Craig Ltd. are to move to a factory on this estate as also British Timken, a division of the Timken Roller Bearing Co. Negotiations with two other firms are at an advanced stage and others are in prospect.

With the advent of motor vehicles some firms began to specialise in motor engineering. Among the pioneers were Andrew M. Goldie, Andrew Young and Robert Blackadder. Andrew M. Goldie added motor engineering to his other activities in 1909. Three years later Andrew Young began business in Chapel Street whence he moved to Mill Street. In 1913 Robert Blackadder built in South Biggar Road the premises which, greatly extended, are now occupied by Laidlaw Ltd. The Goldie firm moved in 1947 into part of the old Beardmore works in Gartlea Road where until 1953 they carried on motor repair work on a very large scale, employing latterly over 100 men. When they gave up this department of their business the premises were taken over by Baxters Bus Services Ltd. for a bus garage.

It was an easy transition for the coachbuilding firms such as Fleming and Taylor and R. Angus and Sons to take up motor body work.

In the years immediately following the first World War a number of operators began bus services between Clarkston and Glasgow. Many people will remember Hendry's buses with

MOTOR BUS OF THE 1920s

solid rubber tyres lurching and squelching their way through
Airdrie's main street at the time when Glasgow Corporation
were relaying the tramway as double-track in 1924-5. Hendry
was a Coatbridge-based operator. The Airdrie man who became
outstanding in the motor bus industry was John C. Sword. He
started in a humble way with four buses running between
Coatbridge and Kilsyth. From this he gradually developed
Midland Bus Services Ltd. which reputedly came to operate a
fleet of 400 vehicles and finally became Western S.M.T. In
Airdrie he started with small premises, formerly Spence's
brass foundry, in Louden Street, then expanded into the County
Garage in Gartlea Road (now the site of the bus stance) and
also the former Blackadder garage in South Biggar Road. Later
a very large garage was built in Carlisle Road. The changing
uses of this building are interesting. In 1939 it was converted
into an aircraft factory building wings for Hurricane fighters.
From 1951 until 1954 it was a tobacco processing and cigarette
making factory of Godfrey Phillips Ltd. In 1957 Salts Saltaire
equipped it as a weaving factory and since 1964 it has been a
bonded warehouse of the Lowland Bonding Co. Ltd.

A bus service to Edinburgh was first provided when
Tennant Brothers of Armadale began to run buses between
Bathgate and Glasgow that linked with S.M.T. buses that came

from Edinburgh only as far west as Bathgate. Before 1930 the S.M.T. service had been extended right through to Glasgow. Their large garage in Connor Street was built in 1949.

Buses between Airdrie and Falkirk were started by Marshall of Standburn with his 'Venture' buses. For a short time he also ran a service from Airdrie to Lanark but ultimately these buses went only as far as Newmains. About the same time — the mid 1920s — Alexanders ran buses from Airdrie to Stirling. Marshall's Falkirk service was absorbed into the Alexanders group.

Other local services were those to Greengairs (Brown) to Glenmavis (W. Irvine), to Chapelhall, Newhouse, Salsburgh and Shotts (P. Irvine: Greenshields), to Moffat Mills and Gartness (Baxter). Calderbank, Holytown, Motherwell, Hamilton and Strathaven were served by the Lanarkshire Traction Co. Ltd. and by the Calderbank firm of Currie and Thomson who continued their service down the Irvine valley to Kilmarnock and Ayr.

The railways made no attempt to face the challenge of the buses. In May 1930 passenger services were withdrawn on the L.N.E.R. Slamannan line and in December 1930 on the L.M.S. Newhouse line. The L.M.S. passenger service to Glasgow via Whifflet ceased in May 1943. After providing for some years only a morning and an evening train in each direction to Edinburgh, British Railways withdrew this skeleton service in January 1956. Electrification of the line from Airdrie to Glasgow and Helensburgh and the inception of the Blue Train Service (7 November 1960), taking only 26 minutes from Airdrie to Glasgow Queen Street, quickly attracted travellers back from bus to rail travel. The new buildings of Airdrie South station were opened on 3 April 1970.

On the occasion of the marriage of the Prince of Wales in 1863 John Spence had coined the phrase 'Airdrie's no dune yet'. That had been adopted as the slogan of the centenary celebrations in 1921 and it would appear to have become the credo of successive Town Councils when, despite the discouragements of the inter-war years before 1939 they carried through a remarkable series of community projects — the new Public Library (1925), Wester Moffat Hospital (1927), the Sewage Purification Works (1928 with an extension in 1938), the Public Baths (1935) and Baillies Lane Hostel (1935) besides the provision of much municipal housing. Two extensions of the burgh were made: the first in 1927 added 339 acres, bringing within the burgh its new hospital and the site of the sewage works; a second in 1937 added a further 685 acres. Building of municipal houses under the Housing Acts of 1923 and 1930 went ahead and by the outbreak of war in 1939 almost 2,600 houses had been built and were occupied. After the war building was resumed and yet another burgh extension was secured; it

annexed a further 841 acres and brought the total burghal area
up to 2,909 acres. By 1962 some 7,000 municipal houses had
been built, about 80 per cent of all the houses in the burgh.
With the steady progress of the £15 million housing scheme
that is swallowing up Petersburn Farm the proportion is now
much higher. Municipal houses now number 10,977, but the real
extent of the improvement in Airdrie's housing conditions is
shown by the rising proportion of 3 and 4-roomed houses as
shown by the decennial Census returns.

Year	Total number of houses	Percentage with 3 or 4 rooms
1911	4,873	18
1921	5,067	18
1931	5,651	31.6
1951	7,706	63.4
1961	9,655	75

For all this, of course a heavy price — not wholly assessable
in terms of money — has had to be paid. The fields that used
to exist within a mile radius of Airdrie Cross have almost
completely disappeared under bricks and concrete.

In 1925-26 the foot of Wellwynd was transformed by the
new buildings of Airdrie Savings Bank and the Public Library
and the formation of a worthy approach to the West Parish
church. New municipal houses on the west side of Wellwynd
and in West Kirk Street continued the face lift. Opposite the
library a new Police Building was opened on 28 March 1959.

Now the appearance of the main street, especially in the
Graham Street section, is rapidly changing. The Royal Buildings
(the old Royal Hotel, the Airdrie Inn of 1794) gave ominous
warnings of an intention to resign from public service and had
to be hurriedly evacuated and demolished in 1969; the municipal
departments that occupied it have been scattered temporarily to
premises all over the town. No decision has yet been taken about
utilisation of the site. On the west side of Gartlea Road on the
site of the old 'Caley' station there is in progress a large shopping
development which will incorporate a bus station. Its present
external appearance is viewed with misgivings. On the opposite
side of Gartlea Road the site of the present bus stance and of
the Pavilion picture house (closed September 1970) is to be
covered by another complex including the new Sheriff Court
building; work on this is to begin in 1971.

In Chapel Street drastic changes are in progress with the
building of blocks of flats on the north side of the street.

It has been announced that, after years of procrastination,
building of a new General Hospital in Airdrie will begin in
April 1971 on the site of the old Airdrie House Maternity
Hospital which was vacated in 1962 and demolished about two
years later.

SITE OF SAVINGS BANK BEFORE 1924

AIRDRIE SAVINGS BANK

The increase in population compelled the provision of more school accommodation. All but two of the schools in use at present are of this century. Alexandra School ceased to be used only in 1970 and it is interesting to note that the centre of its facade is still that of the Alexander Academy built in 1849. Clarkston Academy, the gift of William Towers Clark in 1867, was replaced by a modern building in 1926. In the same year it was decided to demolish Albert School (1876) and build a replacement school on its site. Demolition of Victoria School (1876) started in 1933 and the new school was completed in 1936. A new Chapelside School, this time on a different site, was opened in 1969 but it is already too small and four classes have to meet in the old building of 1883. A new Airdrie Academy was opened at Commonhead in 1941; its former building was then added to Airdrie Central School whose roll soon grew to such an extent that both Alexandra and Albert schools had to be pressed into service as annexes. Later this complex of widely separated buildings was named Airdrie High School but this name has now disappeared with the transfer of its pupils and activities to Caldervale School (1970) Airdrie's latest, largest and most expensive school; it cost £1.25 million.

Moreover the shift of population within the burgh that attended the development of municipal housing schemes sprawling over what was once peripheral countryside brought a clamant need for new schools adjacent to new housing — Caldervale High (1970), Dunrobin (1957), Golfhill (1957), Petersburn (1970), St. Andrew's (1957), St. Edward's (1958), St. Serf's (1957) and Tollbrae (1959).

Before 1918 it had not been unusual for children of Roman Catholic parents to attend Airdrie Academy for their secondary education, since both St. Margaret's and All Saints' schools had only primary courses. In 1958 St. Margaret's became a Junior Secondary school and ceased to offer primary courses. Ten years later it became St. Margaret's High School, providing tuition up to O-level. A new all-through comprehensive school for St. Margaret's is to be built in Bore Road; it is hoped that it will be ready for session 1973–4.

As with schools so with churches; expansion of population away from the centre of the burgh has demanded new buildings. In 1952 Jackson church (originally the Free West) moved out to a new hall-church in the Craigneuk housing area; it is now planning to remove to the new Petersburn scheme. Last year the foundation stone was laid for the new St. Columba's church (successor to the Rawyards Mission of the West parish) in the Roughcraig area. Three new Roman Catholic churches have been built, St. Andrew's (1954) in Whinhall, St. Edward's (1967) in Carlisle Road and St. Serf's (1967) in Rawyards.

Since its inception in 1835 Airdrie Savings Bank has shown continuous progress and now has branches in Coatbridge,

ANDERSON STREET BEFORE 1925
From left to right: old Public Library, old Police Building, West Parish
Church. On extreme right, former office of Airdrie Savings Bank.

Whifflet, Bellshill, Baillieston, Shotts, Muirhead and Gartcosh. In 1970 there were 63,324 depositors; their deposits totalled more than £10.6 millions; and the reserve fund amounted to over £1 million. The premises at the corner of Anderson Street and Wellwynd that the bank had bought in 1895 were already too small by 1914 and when war broke out the bank's directors were negotiating the purchase of a site on the corner of Stirling Street and Wellwynd. Erection of the new bank building began in August 1923 and it was opened on 12 November 1925. This marked the start of much-needed improvements in Wellwynd.

The planning of the new savings bank building was the means of re-opening the question of a new building for the public library. The Carnegie Trustees promised a grant of £6,500 which remained dependent on their founder's stipulation that the town

FOOT OF WELLWYND BEFORE 1924
Site of Public Library on the right

should provide a site free of charge. The directors of the savings bank stepped in with the offer of a free site in Wellwynd on part of their feu, together with £1,000 towards the cost of the building provided that the design and materials of its frontage would harmonise with the new bank building. In the end they gave £1,766 so that the library could open free of debt. The official opening was on 25 September 1925. All the facilities of the old building were continued in the new, with the addition of a junior library and a reference room. Since 1925 many changes have been made. In 1951 the lay-out of the whole ground floor was revised in line with developments in the library service. Two years later the museum was modernised. In September 1960 a substantial two-storey extension was opened to accommodate the Reid Library and provide storage space for surplus stock. A gramophone record library was opened in October 1962 in what had been the smaller museum hall. A second two-storey addition, opened in October 1968, provided a much-needed extension to the lending library on the ground floor and an attractive lecture hall on the upper floor.

AIRDRIE PUBLIC LIBRARY

Significantly each improvement in the library has been followed by increased borrowing out of proportion to any increase in population. In 1921 books issued numbered 59,444; in 1931 issues rose to 123,188, in 1961 to 224,640 and in 1970 to 301,222.

To the utmost of its capacity the public library provided accommodation for meetings of local societies and adult education classes; the modernised museum hall became widely used for exhibitions of painting and photography, including some of the touring exhibitions sponsored by the Scottish Arts Council. In short the building became the cultural focus of Airdrie and the surrounding district. Naturally the idea developed that Airdrie ought to have an Arts Centre and the Town Council were persuaded to experiment by converting for that purpose the old library building in Anderson Street just vacated by the Employment Exchange which had occupied it since 1927. Clever adaptation of the structure converted the former museum hall into a theatre seating 180; what had been the librarian's house became dressing rooms; the old lending library and the reading room became respectively a restaurant and a large practice room with a small club room adjoining. The

GRAMOPHONE RECORD LIBRARY

Arts Centre was opened on 4 October 1967. Its success was immediate. It was now possible to present Arts Council concerts but, much more important, existing Airdrie societies received fresh stimulus and new societies were formed. In the winter of 1970–71 the Centre housed Airdrie Old Union Band (founded 1819), Airdrie and Coatbridge Amateur Operatic Society (1909), Monklands Art Club (1948), Airdrie Arts Guild Dramatic Section (1967), Children's Creative Drama Group (1969), Airdrie Arts Guild Junior Drama Workshop (1970), Philomel Singers (1968) and Airdrie Arts Guild Brass Consort (1970). Within three years from its opening the Arts Centre has proved too small. Plans are under discussion for an extension.

In 1949 Airdrie was selected by the Bureau of Current Affairs for a community experiment designed 'to discover whether the community of a medium-sized town such as Airdrie could be induced to study itself'. At the inaugural meeting on 7 June 1949 the suggestion was thrown out that the community might aim at mounting an exhibition in the autumn of 1950. The idea was seized upon: it was almost the only thing that anyone could understand in the spate of quasi-educational, quasi-philosophical jargon that flowed over them. In this *Airdrie Experiment* it soon became evident that its citizens were more

MUSEUM HALL

ARTS CENTRE THEATRE

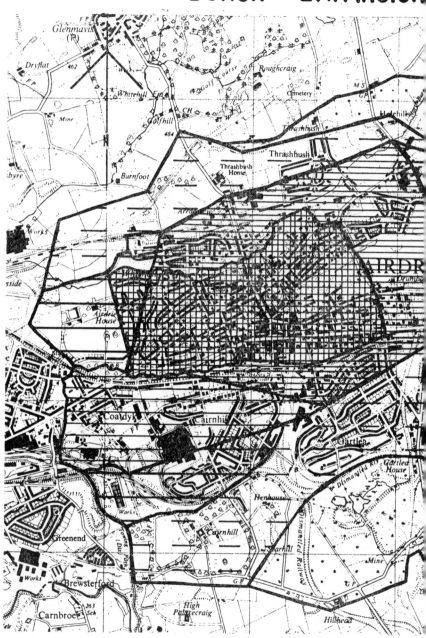

1821 – 1971

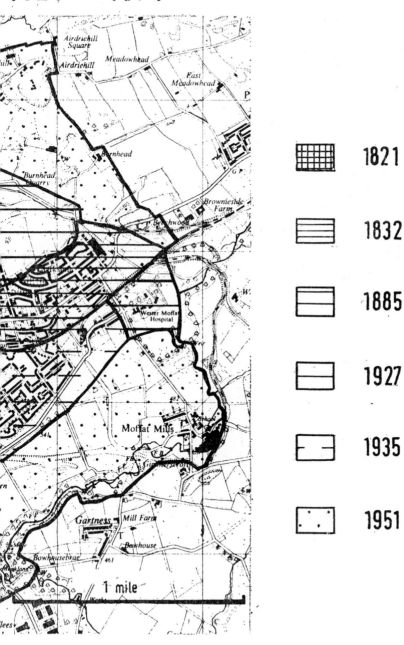

1821

1832

1885

1927

1935

1951

interested in discovering how Airdrie and its traditions had
come about than in forecasting whither it was going. Either
native caution or mathematical awareness made them chary of
extrapolation. Various discussion groups were formed and some
working groups and in due course the *Discovering Airdrie*
exhibition filled the Town Hall for the fortnight beginning 13
October 1950 and was visited by 38,794 persons; the total
population of Airdrie men, women and children was just over
30,000. It had been agreed that the results of the Experiment
should not only be put on exhibition but should also be given
more permanence in a book. And so *The Book of Airdrie* was
prepared by twenty-four writers and seven artists. Two thousand
copies were printed in 1954. Seventeen years later copies are
at a premium and requests—one might almost say petitions—for
copies come in regularly from expatriate Airdrieonians. The
Airdrie Experiment, if it did nothing more, demonstrated the
strength of community spirit that still existed in Airdrie despite
the fact that so many of her citizens had to travel out of the
town to work.

The greatest test of our sense of community is still to
come. Is it strong enough to survive the further centralisation
that is threatened in the plans for re-organisation of local
government?

VIGILANTIA

'I've a richt tae be here' says the cock
  Frae the tap o' the toun's bit o' Latin
'Ma mither kent fine when she ettled tae clock
  This was a guid ferm toun she sat in
An' I mind o' the days o' the mercat an' a'
  An' the Sooth Causey luckenbooths lively an' braw
An' the feein' an' nifferin', daffin' an' jaw
  An' the howffs a' the thrapples got wat in.

'Frae fermin' an' weavin' tae onyx an' art
  The brae has been stey, as ye'll ken,
But I'm prood o' the folk that hae aye dune their part
  An' (mind, I'm no crowin') the men
Wha, like a guid weathercock, faced ilka blast
  An' gied us a future as weel as a past —
An' gin ye should weary an' dover at last,
  I'll skreich till ye're waukened again.'

MADELEINE ORR ARMOUR
(from *The Book of Airdrie*)

LIST OF PROVOSTS

1. 1821 William Mack
2. 1823 Dr James Tennent
3. 1824 James Graham
4. 1825 Dr James Tennent
5. 1827 James Orr
6. 1829 Alexander Galloway
7. 1831 Aitchison Alexander Mack
8. 1832 John Anderson
9. 1833 John Baillie
10. 1834 Matthew Forsyth
11. 1836 David Chapman
12. 1839 George More Nisbet
13. 1842 Walter Rankin
14. 1845 John Wilson Jr.
15. 1848 James Thomson Rankin Jr.
16. 1856 John Davidson
17. 1859 Charles Hendrie
18. 1862 James Forrester
19. 1868 Robert Hamilton
20. 1874 Archibald Cowie
21. 1880 John Black
22. 1883 Gavin Black Motherwell
23. 1889 Alexander Rankin
24. 1890 Robert Adam
25. 1893 George Arthur
26. 1896 James Connor
27. 1899 David Martyn
28. 1905 James Knox
29. 1911 John Orr
30. 1914 Alexander Frew
31. 1921 John Kennedy
32. 1924 Thomas Armour
33. 1930 Gavin Black Motherwell Jr.
34. 1933 John Macfarlane
35. 1936 David Gray
36. 1945 David M. Bonner
37. 1949 Alexander Black
38. 1952 James Walker
39. 1955 William McLenachan
40. 1958 Catherine S. Morton
41. 1961 Alexander Campbell
42. 1964 Thomas Connor
43. 1965 John Donnelly
44. 1968 Thomas W. Macfarlane

OLD POLICE BUILDINGS

OLD BURGH COURT HALL

BAKER'S CART

ONE-CYLINDER RIDLEY CAR
Photographed in 1911 with Andrew Young at the wheel

WEST END OF AIRDRIE WITH WAR MEMORIAL

MONKLAND HOUSE
On the left the old dovecot that was demolished about 1938

ACKNOWLEDGMENTS

Collection of the material from which a selection has been made for this essay has extended over some twenty years. Over that period many people have put me in their debt and it is a pleasure to acknowledge now my especial gratitude to the following: my wife for patient forbearance; the staff of the Historical Search Room of the Scottish Record Office for facilities provided there; Mr J. F. Crichton, Mr A. B. Charteris and Mr I. Macfarlane, successive editors of the *Airdrie and Coatbridge Advertiser* for access to the files of their newspaper; Mr James Taylor, our Town Clerk, for access to Town Council minutes; and Mr W. Scobbie for access to the Local Collection in our Public Library.

Most of the illustrations have been selected from that Local Collection. Airdrie Savings Bank made available the blocks for illustrations 18, 21, 22 and 24; numbers 9 and 34 are from photographs by the *Airdrie Advertiser;* Andrew Muir has kindly provided two new drawings, numbers 1 and 23; his skill is recognised also in numbers 4 and 30 which are from the *Book of Airdrie.* The map has been specially prepared by the Burgh Architect's department.

Finally, the production of the booklet owes much to the helpfulness and courtesy of Mr Alan Crichton and of the technical and printing staff of Messrs George Outram & Co. Ltd., at heir Airdrie printing office.